China

by Joyce Markovics

Consultant: Marjorie Faulstich Orellana, PhD
Professor of Urban Schooling
University of California, Los Angeles

BEARPORT
PUBLISHING

New York, New York

Credits

TOC, © PinkBlue/Shutterstock; 4, © Songquan Deng/Shutterstock; 5L, © NH/Shutterstock; 5R, © Ke Wang/Shutterstock; 7, © TonyV3112/Shutterstock; 8, © laurikin/Shutterstock; 8–9, © Vichly44/iStock; 9R, © Jakrit Jiraratwaro/Shutterstock; 10, © javarman/Shutterstock; 11, © antpkr/Shutterstock; 12–13, © Sean Pavone/Shutterstock; 13, © sevenke/Shutterstock; 14, © Chinaview/Shutterstock; 15, © Lan Images/Shutterstock; 16, © VanHart/Shutterstock; 17, © Jing Aiping/Shutterstock; 18L, © Chunni4691/Shutterstock; 18R, © Snvv/Shutterstock; 19, © Olga Markova/Shutterstock; 20, © Jiang Hongyan/Shutterstock; 21, © Kh.Arty/Shutterstock; 21B, © WebCat/Shutterstock; 22, © windmoon/Shutterstock; 23, © Chinaview/Shutterstock; 24–25, © Yuri Yavnik/Shutterstock; 25, © hecke61/Shutterstock; 26–27, © cyo bo/Shutterstock; 28–29, © Hung Chung Chih/Shutterstock; 30T, © Fourleaflover/Shutterstock; 30M, © lendy16/Shutterstock; 30B, © viphotos/Shutterstock; 31 (T to B), © Sean Pavone/Shutterstock, © Alan49/Shutterstock, © Snvv/Shutterstock, © Sergei Bachlakov, © michel xu/Shutterstock, and © Juhku/Shutterstock; 32, © Noppanisa/Shutterstock.

Publisher: Kenn Goin
Senior Editor: Joyce Tavolacci
Creative Director: Spencer Brinker
Design: Debrah Kaiser

Special thanks to Robert Faulstich for his help reviewing this book.

Library of Congress Cataloging-in-Publication Data

Markovics, Joyce L.
  China / by Joyce Markovics.
      pages cm. — (Countries we come from)
  Includes bibliographical references and index.
  Audience: Ages 4–8.
  ISBN 978-1-62724-858-7 (library binding) — ISBN 1-62724-858-7 (library binding)
  1. China—Juvenile literature. I. Title.
  DS706.M299 2016
  951—dc23
                                    2015004746

For more information, write to Bearport Publishing Company, Inc., 45 West 21st Street, Suite 3B, New York, New York 10010. Printed in the United States of America.

10 9 8 7 6 5 4

Contents

This Is China

HUGE

4

Colorful

Ancient

China is a big country in Asia.

It has more people than any other country.

More than one billion people live there.

China is about the same size as the United States.

7

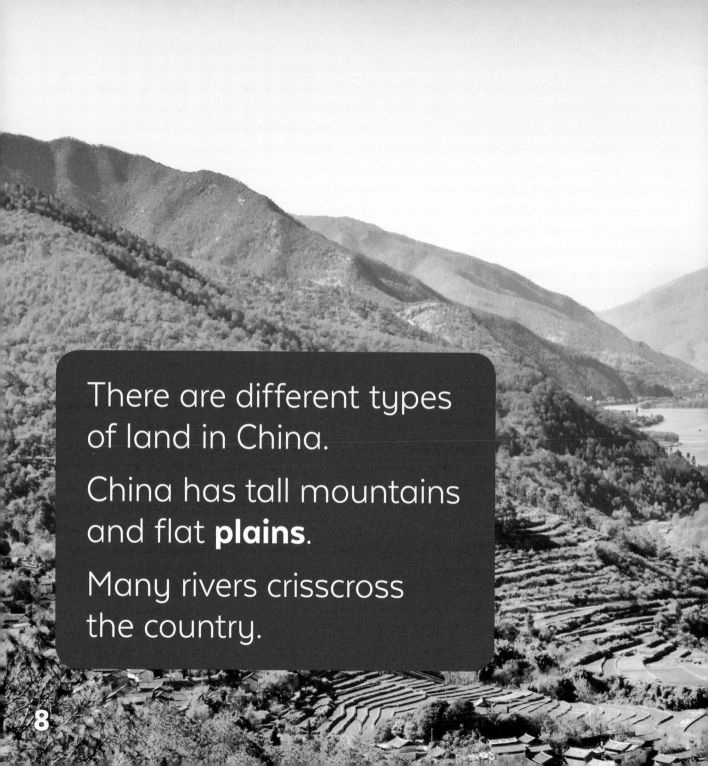

There are different types of land in China.

China has tall mountains and flat **plains**.

Many rivers crisscross the country.

The longest river is called the Yangtze (YANG-SEE). It flows for more than 3,900 miles (6,276 km).

Yangtze River

rice growing on terraces

Farmers grow food on plains and **terraces**.

Terraces are flat fields cut into hills.

China's main **crop** is rice.

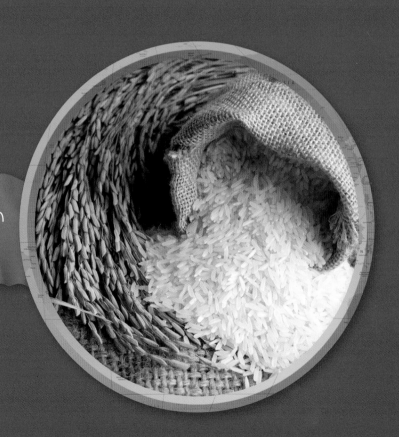

Many Chinese people live in Beijing (BEY-JING).

It's the **capital** of China.

Beijing has many tall buildings.
It's the second-largest city in the country.

The largest city is Shanghai. It has some of the world's tallest buildings.

Many languages are spoken
in China.

Most people speak Mandarin.

More people speak
Mandarin than any
other language in
the world.

This is how you say *hello* in Mandarin:

Nǐ hǎo (nee HAOW)

This is how you say *thank you*:

Xiè xie (SYEH SYEH)

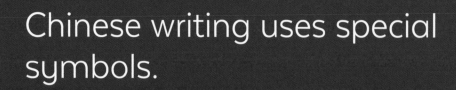

Chinese writing uses special symbols.

Each symbol stands for a word.

Here are the Chinese symbols for *girl* and *boy*:

(girl)　　(boy)

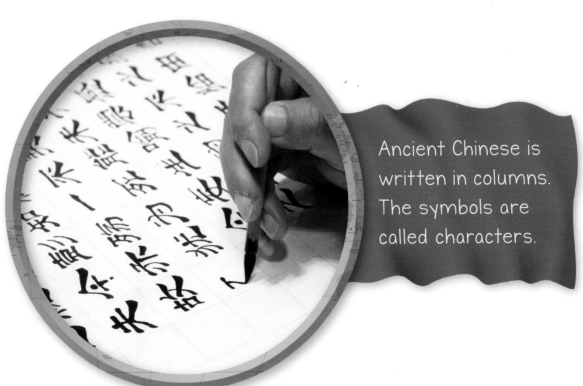

Ancient Chinese is written in columns. The symbols are called characters.

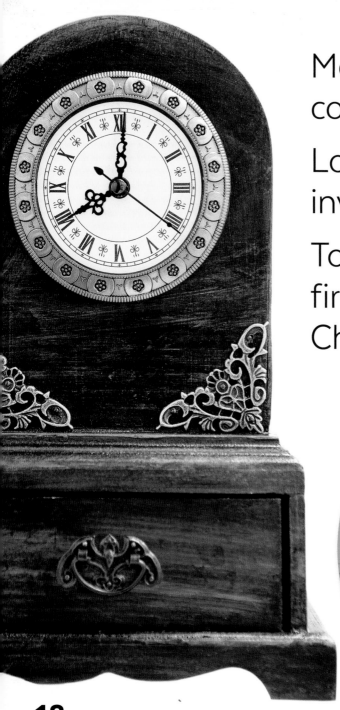

Many **inventions** come from China.

Long ago, clocks were invented there.

Toilet paper and fireworks come from China, too!

Noodles were invented in China 4,000 years ago.

People in China eat many kinds of food.

Dumplings are very popular.

They are dough stuffed with vegetables or meat.

chopsticks

Chinese people often use chopsticks to eat their food.

Lots of holidays are celebrated in China.

One of them is Chinese New Year.

People dance with big paper dragons.

Children carry red lanterns and march in **parades**.

lantern

Red is a very lucky color in China.

There is a huge, ancient wall in China.

It stretches thousands of miles.

It was built to keep out enemies.

Millions of people visit the Great Wall each year. They come from all over the world.

The fastest train in the world is in China.

It's the Shanghai maglev train.

The train uses super-strong magnets to float above its tracks.

The Shanghai maglev train can go more than 300 miles per hour (483 kph).

What else is special about China?

It's the only place where giant pandas live in the wild!

These big animals are loved by the Chinese people.

bamboo

Pandas eat a type of grass called bamboo.

Fast Facts

Capital city:
Beijing

Population of China:
More than 1.35 billion

Main language:
Mandarin

Money: Yuan (yoo-AHN)

Major religions: Buddhism, Taoism, Christianity, and Islam

Neighboring countries include:
Russia, Vietnam, India, and Mongolia

Cool Fact: The most popular hobby in China is stamp collecting.

capital (KAP-uh-tuhl) a city where a country's government is based

crop (KROP) a plant that is grown for food

inventions (in-VEN-shuhnz) new things that people have created

parades (puh-RADES) groups of people walking together as part of a ceremony or festival

plains (PLAYNZ) large, flat areas of land

terraces (TER-iss-iz) raised, flat platforms of land with sloping sides

Index

Read More

Branscombe, Allison. *All About China: Stories, Songs, Crafts, and More for Kids.* North Clarendon, VT: Tuttle Publishing (2014).

Jenner, Caryn. *Welcome to China (DK Readers).* New York: DK (2008).

Learn More Online

To learn more about China, visit
www.bearportpublishing.com/CountriesWeComeFrom

About the Author

Joyce Markovics lives far from China in Tarrytown, New York. However, she still enjoys Peking opera, dim sum, and kung fu.